THE TRUE COST OF TOYS

HOW TO SHOP TO CHANGE THE WORLD

MARY COLSON

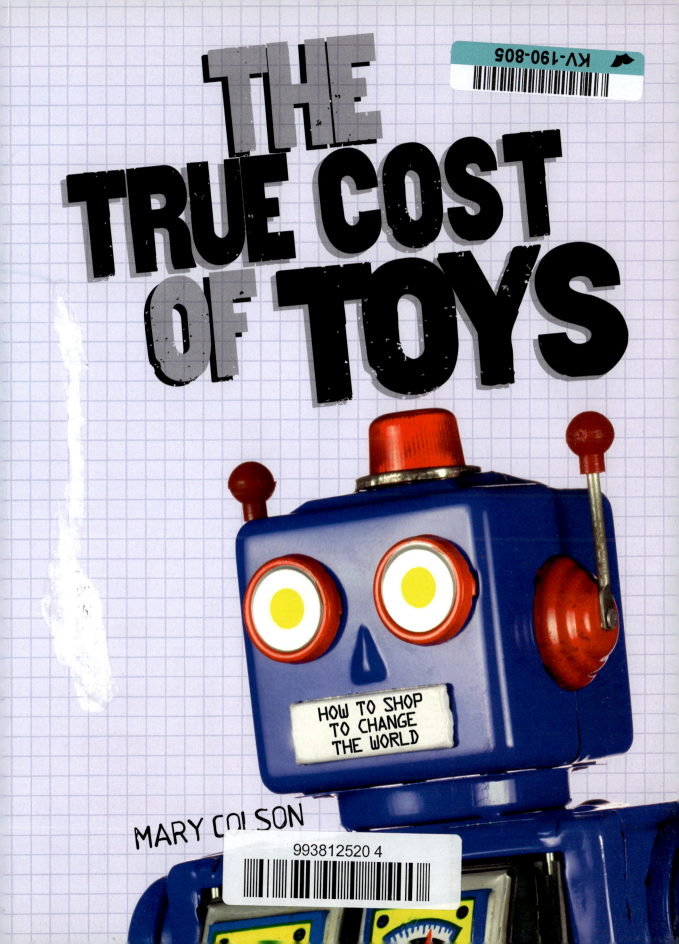

Published in paperback in 2014 by Wayland
Copyright © Wayland 2014

Wayland
338 Euston Road
London NW1 3BH

Wayland Australia
Level 17/207 Kent Street
Sydney, NSW 2000

Picture acknowledgements
Corbis: Pallava Bagla 20, Costa007 8t, Rahat Dar/EPA 41, Macduff Everton 25t,
Imaginechina 12, Lucas Schifres/Visuals Unlimited 22, Joe Tan/Reuters 18t; Dreamstime:
Bpperry 13, Danielal 39b, Kudrashka-a 38, Monkey Business Images 11t, 37b, Moutwtrng 33t,
Ngarto 44, Photo25th 11b, Portokalis 35, Uptall 10, Vladb 31, Yummyyui 15t, Zatletic 40;
Forest Stewardship Council: 27t; Shutterstock: Alexkatkov 9b, BartlomiejMagierowski 7t,
19, 23, Hung Chung Chih 45, Coprid 6b, Szasz-Fabian Ilka Erika 2, Evikka 8b, Stephanie Frey
4m, Mandy Godbehear 21b, Gwoeii 24, Marke H. 36b, Hal P 37tl, Panyanon Hankhampa 29tl,
Irin K 4br, KellyBoreson 30t, Paul McKinnon 34, Tatiana Morozova 25b, Paha_l 42, Pavel L
Photo and Video 5b, 36t, 39t, Pressmaster 43, Rangizzz 8m, Dr. Morley Read 26, 27b, ROMA
21t, Shutswis 4l, 6m, Suwit 28, Thefinalmiracle 18b, Tracing Tea 30b, Trainman32 29tr,
Hor Jorgen Udvang 33b, Kiselev Andrey Valerevich 5t, Wandee007 7b, Ivonne Wierink 6t,
Zurijeta 32; Traidcraft: 14, 16, 17; Wikipedia: Siavash Ghazvinian 15b.

A catalogue record for this book is available from the British Library.

ISBN: 978 0 7502 8345 8
Printed in China
10 9 8 7 6 5 4 3 2 1

Wayland is a division of Hachette
Children's Books,
an Hachette UK company.

www.hachette.co.uk

CONTENTS

THE TRUTH BEHIND TOYS

When you shop for the latest toy in an Aladdin's cave of a toy shop, do you think about how what you buy might affect people elsewhere in the world? Do you ever wonder where your toy has come from? What about your model kit or board game? What's behind the shiny metal, moving parts, flashing lights and coloured plastic?

Dying for toys

The toy industry is an US$83 billion dollar global giant. All over the world there is a high demand for toys, with a particular rush around Christmas. In order to meet this demand, there is a human and environmental cost. Toys may look cute and cuddly but what lies beneath the fur and the fluff? Child labour, worker deaths, **suicides** and eco-disasters are just some of the hidden costs of our treasured toys.

Exciting toys can help to develop our imaginations, but do you know what your toys are made of and where they come from?

4

What's a sweatshop?

Many toy factories are in countries where the laws are very different from those in Europe or North America. People in these factories work very long hours for very little pay. Their working conditions are often hazardous. For example, poor **ventilation** in some factories causes workers to fall ill from the heavy fumes of glues and **chemicals**. These kinds of factories are called **sweatshops**. Sometimes children work in them, too.

Many children enjoy a childhood full of toys but, the children who work in toy factories have no such freedom.

People power

This book will scratch beneath the surface, go beyond the beautifully packaged toys we buy, and examine the links between supply, demand, labour conditions, and environmental issues such as manufacturing and waste. It will also look at companies with **ethical practices** that are helping to make things better all the way along the **supply chain**. It will show that you have the power to be an **ethical consumer** and shop to change the world.

SHOP TO CHANGE THE WORLD

When you buy things in a shop, you are called a **consumer**. You decide what you buy and what you consume. The toys you buy and the money you spend affect people elsewhere. There's a whole network and supply chain to ensure that the products you want arrive on the shop shelves. You have the power to shop to change the world. Your actions could help to change conditions for the better in toy factories all over the world.

Taking your pick from shelves stacked high with toys is every child's dream, but have you ever thought about who makes these toys and what lives they lead?

5

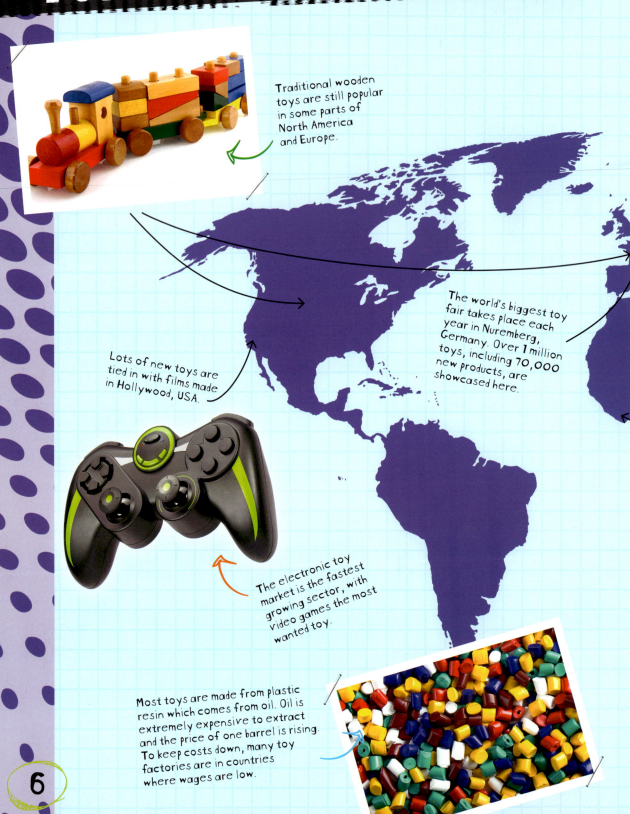

Traditional wooden toys are still popular in some parts of North America and Europe.

Lots of new toys are tied in with films made in Hollywood, USA.

The world's biggest toy fair takes place each year in Nuremberg, Germany. Over 1 million toys, including 70,000 new products, are showcased here.

The electronic toy market is the fastest growing sector, with video games the most wanted toy.

Most toys are made from plastic resin which comes from oil. Oil is extremely expensive to extract and the price of one barrel is rising. To keep costs down, many toy factories are in countries where wages are low.

There are many toy factories in the cities of Shenzhen and Guangzhou in Guangdong Province, China.

In Europe, 20% of toys are bought for children below the age of 5.

The Asian toy market is the fastest growing in the world.

The consumer toy market in Japan is worth US$6 billion per year.

The city of Dongguan near Hong Kong has over 4,000 toy factories.

China makes 80% of the toys sold worldwide. Most are made in Guangdong Province, where US$12 billion worth of toys are produced every year.

Taiwan is a large video game manufacturer along with the USA.

Lots of the rubber used in toy manufacture comes from rubber tree plantations in Liberia, West Africa.

CHAPTER 1

GLOBAL TRADE

Toys are part of the magic of childhood. They allow us to play as well as nurture our imaginations, develop our skills and help us to learn to socialise with others. Think about the toys you've played with since you were little: dolls, dressing-up clothes, tea sets, farm animals, diggers, battery-powered toys, clockwork toys. Where did they all come from? Who made them? What's their toy story?

When you buy a toy in a shop. it is the end of a long chain. Your toy began life a long time before you owned it. But what is this chain?

What is a supply chain?

A supply chain is made up of all the individuals, businesses and resources involved in creating a product, from **raw materials** to finished merchandise. The chain begins with supplying the raw materials and ends with the consumer buying the product. All your toys will have been part of a supply chain..

The enormous toy industry caters for children of all ages.

The toy supply chain

1. Natural resources, such as oil, are extracted.

2. The natural resources are transported to a factory to be processed (for example into plastic).

3. At a toy factory, designers will work on the look, shape and style of the toy.

6. Workers package the toys carefully into boxes ready for shipping.

5. Assembly lines manufacture thousands of copies of the toy.

4. The plastic is then transported to the toy factory for colouring and moulding into the required shape.

7. The boxes are distributed to toy shops all over the world.

8. The **retailer** stocks the toys on the shelves.

9. The consumer buys the toy and takes it home.

Oil extraction from oil wells such as this one use up valuable resources and can damage the environment.

Children in China spend around US$6 a year on toys compared to a child in the USA spending US$34, almost six times as much.

SUPPLY AND DEMAND

Over 70% of the world's toys have 'Made in China' stamped on them. Of all the toys sold in Europe, 85% are made in China. This means that China is the biggest supplier of toys in the world. Europe and North America are the largest markets so they 'demand' the most toys.

SUPPLY AND DEMAND

All businesses have to make money and toy companies are no different. They need to make a **profit** to pay for wages, resources and factory costs. The toy factories want to make and supply enough toys to meet the consumer demand for them. The more toys they sell, the more profit they make. If they make too many toys and people don't want them, the company will lose money. If there aren't enough toys available, again, the company will lose money so they try to supply enough to meet demand.

This balance is an important part of any business, particularly in the toy industry where some toys are fashionable only for a short time and new toys and games are being created all the time.

From warehouses like this one in China, thousands of different toys are sent all over the world.

Business sense

Like all businesses, toy companies want to make as much money as possible so they set up their factories in countries where the wages are low, such as China, India or Indonesia. The governments of these countries want jobs for their workers so they make it easy for foreign businesses to set up factories there. This way, the host country gets lots of jobs for their workers and the foreign toy business doesn't have to pay such high labour costs. This seems to make good business sense, but at what cost to the quality of the products and the quality of life for the workers who make them?

Decisions made in the head offices of toy companies can affect the lives of workers on the factory floor thousands of miles away.

CONSUMER NATION

What are the pros and cons of a company setting up a toy factory in the Far East?

Pros

Lower wage costs means cheaper toys for consumers in Europe and North America.

Fewer labour laws mean people can work longer and more toys are produced.

Making toys in another country means that you have access to another market of consumers who might want to buy your product.

Cons

There are fewer jobs in the toy industry in North America and Europe.

The issue of poor working conditions in the toy factories is hidden away.

If someone investigates factory conditions, the human sweatshop problem simply moves to a place where wages are even lower.

Imagine being a worker in a toy factory, making the same thing over and over again.

QUALITY CONTROL?

Toy company bosses in, say, North America, want their supply chains to work smoothly and efficiently. Chinese factory owners want the toy company to use them to make their goods so they bid for the work. This usually means promising to make thousands of toys, for example, such as board games, for a very low price. The toy company bosses want to maximise their profits so they agree. And because the factory is thousands of miles away in another country, they don't have to look too carefully at the reality of the working conditions for the people who are making the products.

Complex chain

As we've seen, there is often a long chain that separates the toy company from the factory where the toy is actually made. There may be dozens of links in the supply chain so as well as monitoring working conditions, checking on product quality can also be difficult. (See page 32 for stories about toy recalls.)

SUPPLY AND DEMAND

There are so many toy factories that smaller ones can be overlooked and less carefully monitored by the authorities. This means that poor conditions or illegal working practices are able to continue.

Workers on a production line at a toy factory in Guangzhou, Guangdong Province, in southern China.

In a global **economy**, supply chain management often includes dealings with companies and individual contributors in other countries. This might require obeying different laws or paying rent for factory space. It may also mean there are different quality standards and regulations. This can be true for the toys themselves but also for the working conditions of the employees.

Products, not people

Foreign toy companies are able to 'assume' that pay and conditions are acceptable to the workers because they are far away and they're not directly employing the people. In countries like China, workers may have few rights. Many foreign business owners are happy for the factories to produce as many toys as they can, whatever conditions the workers may have to endure. As long as nothing disrupts the manufacturing process and affects the profits, then nothing changes. Getting the products made quickly and shipped to retailers and consumers elsewhere is the only goal.

How could things change?

Campaigners say that the quality control of the toy industry could be improved tomorrow if the world's big toy companies accepted making less profit in favour of creating a fairer supply chain.

Some toy factories in China provide housing for their workers, but often this accommodation is poor.

13

WORKING FOR CHANGE

So who do you think is responsible for keeping things as they are? Let's take a look at some companies and organisations who are trying to make a difference and what you can do to make trade fairer and improve working conditions around the world.

It's clear that toy companies, governments of developed and developing countries, factory owners, and toy consumers like us, all have a part to play in keeping things the way they are. But if just one of us decides to join a larger movement for change, then eventually an improvement will be seen on the factory floor.

A fair deal

Traidcraft is an ethical business that works with communities all over the world and ensures that each stage of the supply chain is fair and **eco-friendly**. Traidcraft guarantees that its partner toy makers in India can be sure that they will get proper workshop facilities and a fair day's pay for a fair day's work. Traidcraft doesn't employ child workers and it makes sure that its employees get proper breaks.

The toys are sold in shops and through catalogues in the UK. By limiting stores, the company distributes products direct, to save on shipping costs.

Some companies, such as Traidcraft, sell ethical and eco-friendly toys.

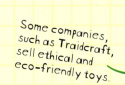

Investing in communities

Traidcraft gives the toy makers a fair share of their profits. These are then re-invested into the community to improve living conditions for everyone. It fulfills Traidcraft's mission of fighting poverty through trade and it's a great example of how a supply chain can work fairly and ethically.

Children helping children

One day in 1995, 12-year-old Craig Kielburger was reading his local newspaper. In it, he read a story about a child worker in Pakistan who had been killed for daring to speak out against child labour. Craig was so shocked, he founded the charity Free the Children which campaigns against child labour around the world. Today, Craig's charity works with young people in many countries to raise awareness, and funds education programmes for young people.

SHOP TO CHANGE THE WORLD

You can choose to buy Traidcraft toys and show your support for ethical business. You are saying 'no' to child labour and 'no' to poor working conditions in sweatshops. For more information, go to www.traidcraft.co.uk.

Campaigner against child labour, Craig Kielburger speaks to students at a We Day event in Waterloo, Canada. We Day is a day to inspire school children to care about social issues, such as poverty and child labour, and to act to make a difference.

WHAT IS FAIR TRADE?

Toy makers around the world, from Sri Lanka and Vietnam to India and China, benefit from working with **fair trade** organisations. Many Western consumers will only buy toys from companies that have the 'fair trade' logo. What is fair trade and how can people power make a difference in the toy industry?

A fair deal

Fair trade is a way of buying and selling goods at a fair price. It aims to stop poor workers being **exploited** by making sure that the people who make the goods get a fair slice of the profit. It has transformed the lives of many workers in poorer countries by enabling them to use their skills and talents to trade their way out of poverty.

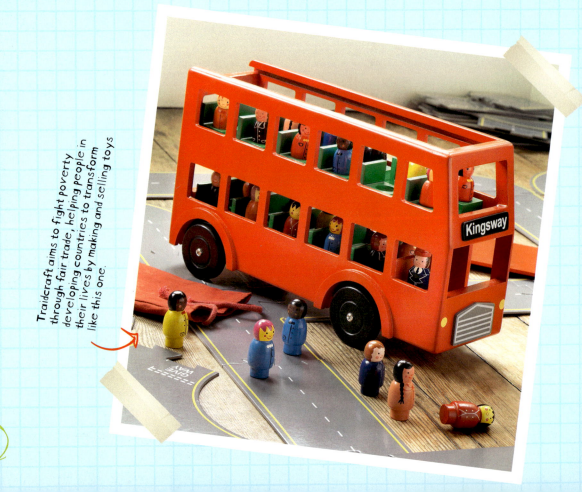

Traidcraft aims to fight poverty through fair trade, helping people in developing countries to transform their lives by making and selling toys like this one.

An ethical approach

By investing some profits back into the communities where the toys are made, fair trade helps to build professional businesses where workers have rights and protection. The factory owners look after their workers and make sure they are healthy and well paid. Some fair trade businesses even use the profits to build good housing for their workers or build wells for easy access to drinking water.

Pressure groups

There are many campaign groups that work to bring about big changes in the general toy supply chain (see page 47). The Toy Safety Campaign is supported by the European Union and is concerned with working conditions as well as the safety of materials used to make the toys themselves.

CONSUMER NATION

Lots of people sign **petitions** and join a campaign, but what are the pros and cons of this?

Pros

You can use your voice to speak up for those who can't.

You can experience how your own consumer power can change the world and see real results.

You can help to make a difference to workers' lives.

Cons

You might be too young - check out what they offer to youth campaigners.

Don't be disappointed if things don't change quickly. People might not take you seriously because you're young, but that didn't stop Craig Kielburger - be inspired by his example (see page 15).

Campaigners say that if everybody bought fair trade toys, the whole toy industry would start to change for the better.

17

CHAPTER 2

WORKERS' RIGHTS

Who makes the toys we buy and what kind of conditions do they really live and work in? What's it like for children in one country to produce toys they'll never play with, for another country's children to enjoy? We've learned that fair trade seeks to make a difference but how bad are things for the workers? What does 'poor working conditions' really mean?

Toy production, pay and pressure

There seems to be a link between how poor a country is and how exploitable its people are. If there are more people looking for work than jobs available, people will tend to accept any job and work in any conditions.

Children in poorer countries are often forced to work to help their families.

To keep costs low and to make the price of a single toy reasonable, some toy factory owners pay workers based on how many toys they make. The amount of money they get depends on the number of items, such as toy soldiers, dolls or skipping ropes, they complete in their shift. If they want to make enough money to support their families, the workers have to work overtime on top of their already very long shifts.

Workers on a production packing line in a factory in Shenzhen, China. Toy factories employ many people to make their products and meet their targets.

What's a trade union?

Factory workers in the UK, for example, can join a **trade union** which means that they have people representing them and speaking up for their rights. The union leaders will meet with managers and discuss serious issues so that everybody's working environment is safe and positive. In many countries around the world, trade unions are illegal. Sweatshops tend to exist where unions are banned.

SHOP TO CHANGE THE WORLD

It's easy to check online to find out where a toy is made and who made it. There are also lots of campaign groups and journalists interested in the toy industry and the working conditions, so there's lots online to read and learn. It's easy to avoid buying sweatshop-made goods if you just take a few minutes to look. By doing this, you are choosing to say no to sweatshops and yes to a fair supply chain.

CASE STUDY 1

CHILD'S PLAY? THE LIFE OF A CHILD SWEATSHOP WORKER

Research shows that if you were to buy a new football today, there is a good possibility that the ball has been made by someone your age or even younger...

Iqbal works in a factory on the outskirts of the city of Jalandhar in India. The day after his twelfth birthday, he had to leave his home and his parents and look for work in the city. He has four younger brothers and sisters at home and everyone has to help out.

Iqbal walked to the city with the clothes he stood up in and a few spare rupees. He stayed with his cousin for a week while he tried to find work. He was so pleased when he found a job in the football factory. He called his parents to let them know he would soon be sending money home.

Young children are often used to sew the panels of a football together.

He moved into the factory dormitory like most of the workers and for six days a week, Iqbal now stitches football panels together - 32 panels per football. All by hand.

Iqbal earns about 5 cents an hour, depending on how fast he works. Along with around 40 other children, he works 10-15 hour shifts each day. The light isn't good and he finds his eyes get tired staring at the small stitches. By the end of his shift, he is so tired that he pricks his fingers with the needle by mistake.

The football Iqbal is sewing will sell for US$50 in the USA. But Iqbal doesn't know this. He will earn around 59 cents. He's happy to have a job and be able to send money home but he'd rather not have to live in the dirty, cramped dormitory. And the factory supervisor sometimes shouts at him, which he doesn't like. He used to go to school. Sometimes as he's stitching, he tries to remember the major rivers of Pakistan or capital cities of the world.

Iqbal's dream is to one day play football like his heroes Lionel Messi and Cristiano Ronaldo. But mostly he'd just like to go home and see his family.

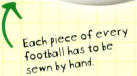

Each piece of every football has to be sewn by hand.

Footballs made by child workers in developing countries are bought by people in more economically developed countries who are often unaware of where or how the balls were made.

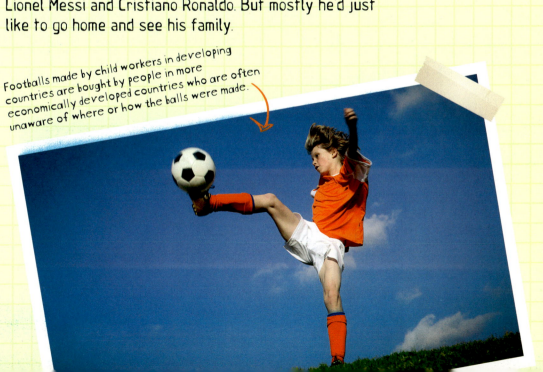

TOYS, TRAFFICKING AND DESPERATION

Iqbal's story, sadly, is not unique. There are thousands of children all over the world working in toy sweatshops. Children are employed in sweatshops because they work for less money and are less likely to complain about poor working conditions – they know no different. An education is out of the question for these children.

Some workers are tied into contracts with job agencies which costs them much of their wages.

SUPPLY AND DEMAND

According to the International Labor Organisation, there are around 220 million child workers between the ages of 5 and 14 in the world. Some are forced to work and kept in **confinement** whilst others are physically abused. Some are even abducted and sold. This is called **human trafficking**. Of these estimated 220 million, Asia has 56% (122 million), Africa 22% (50 million) and South America 22% (50 million).

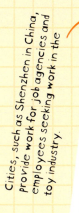
Cities, such as Shenzhen in China, provide work for job agencies and employees seeking work in the toy industry.

Paying a debt

In cities all over Asia, Africa and South America, there are corrupt job agencies. The agents promise to find people work, for example, in the toy industry. There is a fee and a contract to sign. When the hopeful workers are found a job, they are horrified to learn that they have signed a debt contract agreeing to keep paying the agents. This means they have to pay the agency out of their wages, which may mean a huge debt that lasts for many years. Instead of sending money to their families, they are forced to work extra time to meet their debt payments. The United Nations is trying to stop this kind of exploitation but the problem is vast and in an industry like the toy industry, there are always more people willing to sign up for a steady job.

CONSUMER NATION

The sweatshop issue is very complicated. Think about these questions and see if you can come up with some answers.

1. What are the pros and cons of sweatshops - should we just campaign for them all to be shut today?
2. Would it make a lasting difference to the sweatshop workers or would they just go to another industry?
3. How would it affect the cost of the toys we want?
4. Would it make a difference to how quickly we get them?
5. Are you prepared to accept the difference it would make to you and the toys you want?

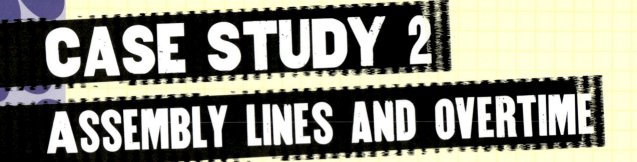

CASE STUDY 2
ASSEMBLY LINES AND OVERTIME

A toy factory in Indonesia. Any day of the week, Fatima works on the assembly line making model cars. In the UK, those cars would sell for over £20 each. They would be 'collectible'. Fatima doesn't earn much of that herself, though.

It's 8 a.m. and Fatima's shift has started. She lives nearby with her husband so she only has a 15-minute bus ride to the factory. She has to work because her husband had an accident in another factory and can't work anymore. Fatima is expecting their first child in a few months' time.

It's peak season now as Christmas approaches in Western countries. She won't get on a bus home till nearly midnight tonight. At least she'll get a few hours' overtime pay. Last month, Fatima worked more than 120 hours extra on top of her shifts and didn't have a single day off. She's only 27 but Fatima is starting to look like an old woman.

For many workers, bus rides to work can be the only time they see daylight.

Life on the assembly line...

Fatima doesn't mind the packing station on the assembly line but she can't stand the paint station. The tiny vehicles are sprayed by hand in a small room at the back of the factory. There aren't any windows and the paint fumes make her feel dizzy and sick. The glue used to stick everything together is strong-smelling, too. Just yesterday, she passed out and had to be taken outside. She lost the whole afternoon's pay because she had left her station without asking for an 'off-duty permit', and is worried about her growing baby.

The factory itself is a run-down old building. The roof leaks during the rains. If she's working overtime, Fatima makes sure she gets a toilet pass before 10p.m. After that, the workers have to use barrels of water as the flushing water is turned off.

The supervisors are strict but the manager is worse. Last week, Fatima made over 900 model cars. She filled in her work log and the manager fined her some of her wages for missing her target. Fatima was so tired she couldn't remember her target but she knows she couldn't have worked any harder or faster.

It's now midnight and Fatima leaves the assembly line for the bus ride home. She is half-asleep on her feet as she walks away.

... is doing the same thing over and over again.

25

CHAPTER 3

TOYS AND TOXINS

Look around your bedroom: what are most of your toys made of? Is it plastic or wood, metal or material? Whatever your toys are made of, the resources required to make them had to be found somewhere. This chapter will look at the environmental and health issues surrounding the resourcing, manufacturing and disposing of toys.

Animals are often displaced and plants and trees destroyed when oil pipelines, such as this one in the Ecuadorian Amazon rainforest, are built.

Harmful to health

Some of the raw materials used to make our toys, such as oil, are extremely **toxic**. This means that they are harmful to human health and other wildlife. Paints, glues and dyes all contain chemicals which can cause serious illnesses if inhaled. The people who work in the toy industry need proper clothing and ventilation if they work with these products, but all too often this isn't the case. **Respiratory** problems, skin conditions and lung illnesses are just some of the consequences for the workers.

Rainforest ruined

One of the planet's most precious resources is the rainforests that circle the Earth's tropical zones. The rainforests absorb carbon dioxide and give out oxygen for us to breathe. Campaigners have pointed out that the rainforests are being cut down at an alarming rate to make way for cattle ranches and crops. The valuable hardwood trees are also used to make furniture and toys.

Most of our toys are made of plastic, so the toy industry needs a lot of oil. Unfortunately for the Amazon rainforest, it is rich in oil deposits. Extracting oil is a messy and expensive activity. In the Ecuadorian Amazon, for example, local people were exposed to toxic oil waste and their lives were changed dramatically. Not only did they become very ill, their towns and villages and rivers were ruined by the thick black poisonous sludge.

The pollution caused by an oil spill in the Ecuadorian Amazon rainforest had a devastating impact on humans and wildlife in the region.

THE RUBBER TAPPING TRADE

Many toys are made from rubber because it's an incredibly versatile material, but do you know where rubber comes from and how it is harvested? Welcome to the rubber plantations of Liberia, in West Africa.

Life on a rubber plantation

Liberia is one of the world's biggest **exporters** of rubber. Life is pretty tough for the people who work on the rubber plantations. Rubber comes from trees and has to be removed or tapped from the trunk. The workers are paid by each cup of rubber they tap off. Each worker is given a target amount of cups to gather, but often their targets are unrealistic. In order to meet the targets, the workers sometimes even bring their children to work as well.

Each cup is poured into a big bucket. When the bucket is full, it is usually the children's job to carry the heavy bucket to the weigh-in station at the farm which can be many miles away. In order to keep the trees healthy, the tappers and their children must spray toxic pesticides onto the trees. This is usually done without any protective clothing or masks, which can lead to serious health problems.

To get rubber from rubber trees, it has to be tapped by making a cut in the tree trunk.

Life as a rubber tapping worker can be hard, working long hours and carrying heavy loads. However, some plantation workers are joining unions to get their voices heard.

Sheets of latex hung out to dry. Latex is used in many toys, such as beach toys, the buttons on games consoles, and paints and glues.

Award-winning union

In the Liberian town of Harbel, the workers at the Firestone rubber plantation decided to make a difference. The workers have joined together in a union and worked with their bosses to ban child labour on the plantation. Through discussions, the bosses also agreed to reduce the rubber targets by 25%. The best result of all, however, is that the bosses agreed to provide all children living on the plantation with better schools.

SHOP TO CHANGE THE WORLD

Want to be an eco-toy warrior? Then check out which companies make their toys from recycled materials. A quick Internet search is all you need to find out and there are loads of companies to choose from. Green Toys™ is just one US company who makes toys from recycled plastic, recycled rubber and other environmentally-friendly materials. On their website, they explain that they don't use harmful chemicals and even their packaging is eco-friendly.

29

COTTON AND CHEMICALS

Think of all the fun you've had dressing up your toys and yourself in different costumes and funny clothes. Most of these costumes require cotton and the toy industry uses a lot of it. But how is the cotton industry organised? Where is it big business? And are the workers and the environment protected?

Life on the cotton farms of Asia

Uzbekistan in Central Asia is the world's largest cotton producer. Around two-thirds of the world's cotton is grown in Asia and is worth billions of dollars. Cotton is one of Uzbekistan's major exports that helps to keep its economy going. Unfortunately, adults and children alike are forced to work in appalling conditions.

Uzbek cotton harvesters are often paid according to how much cotton they pick.

30

Child slavery

Nearly all of Uzbekistan's cotton is harvested by hand.
Human rights groups estimate that hundreds of thousands
of children are forced to work on the plantations. The
cotton harvest begins in September and the government
closes down rural schools so the children can be sent to
work. For three months, children as young as nine or ten
years are forced to pick cotton by hand. They aren't paid
very much - if at all. Each child is given a daily target
of 50kg of cotton. Many become exhausted and ill.
Some even try to run away but they are threatened
with expulsion from school.

SHOP TO CHANGE THE WORLD

The Environmental Justice
Foundation runs campaigns
on behalf of cotton workers
and the environment. You
can find out more about their
campaigning work online at
www.ejfoundation.org.

Environmental impact

The Aral Sea was once a vast inland sea. The cotton industry in
Uzbekistan demands a huge amount of water so about 40 years ago,
cotton farms started taking water from the Aral Sea. Now, decades later,
the Aral Sea has shrunk to the point of no return. The shrinking sea
has an environmental consequence for both the cotton plants and the
country. Salt granules that lie on the exposed sea floor are picked up by
the wind and carried away. As the salt is carried, it acts like a scrubbing
brush, scouring all the plants for hundreds of miles around. Harvests are
reduced because the salt kills the plants. Once the plants have gone,
there's nothing to hold the soil together so the land becomes useless.

An abandoned boat turns
to rust in the dried-up
Aral Sea, Uzbekistan.

CASE STUDY 3

CAUTION: THIS TOY MAY HARM YOUR HEALTH!

Maria works for a large toy company in the USA. She's based in the public relations department. Mostly she gets calls from customers complaining about a toy. Those calls are easy to solve: it's either a refund or a replacement. Last week, though, she had a really bad call.

A four-year-old boy had been playing with a toy made by her company and then become ill. His parents rushed him to hospital and the doctors found that he had lead poisoning. It had come from the paint on the toy.

Over the next few days, Maria and her colleagues had a lot of calls from worried parents whose children had also become poorly playing with these toys. Maria told her boss and the company recalled the toys.

Recalling toys is a big deal. Notices are put in newspapers, online, and even read out on national radio and news stations. Maria and her colleagues write the press releases and take questions from journalists. The company wants to do the right thing and protect children.

Some factories have good quality controls and regular inspections.

Shiny toy cars need the proper paint applied to them, to ensure they are safe for children to play with.

Over the next few weeks, thousands of toys are recalled. Customers get their money back and the toys are examined. The USA has strict laws about toy safety. Paint can only have 0.6% lead in it because it is harmful to humans. Lead poisoning can lead to behavioural problems and learning difficulties. The paint on the toys is found to have too much lead in it. The children have sucked on the toys, swallowed the paint and become ill.

The company now needs to work out where in the supply chain the quality control systems failed. A large review takes place which takes many months. The supply chain is so large and complex and it takes time for systems to change. The children recover and no lasting damage is done - this time.

A factory worker spray paints component parts on a factory assembly line.

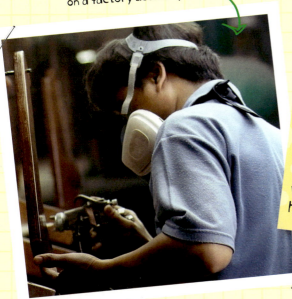

SHOP TO CHANGE THE WORLD

In the USA, the Consumer Product Safety Commission investigates all cases of toy recall. Sometimes, toy companies are fined if the commission discovers they are to blame. In 2009, the European Union created a law which stated that all toys imported or sold within the EU must be free from harmful chemicals. The Toy Safety Directive has already made a huge difference to the international toy supply chain. China has improved its supervision of toy factories and has closed down over 700 companies which it found to be using poor quality or harmful materials in their toys.

WASTE MATTERS

Like all large-scale manufacturing industries, the toy industry creates its fair share of waste. Christmas time is the busiest time of the year for toy factories and retailers so this is when the rubbish pile peaks. It's estimated that each year in the UK, 13 million old, unwanted toys go into landfill sites.

Of course, at Christmas time, if you're lucky, you will get a whole lot of new toys to play with. So what do you do with the old ones?

CONSUMER NATION

What are the pros and cons of recycling your own toys rather than throwing them out?

Pros

There's less waste going into landfill sites.
Charities can pass your old toys on to people who will enjoy playing with them.
You'll feel good about giving to others and being eco-friendly.

Cons

Not everything can be recycled or passed on. Some toys, such as jigsaws, may have missing pieces, or be broken beyond repair.
It takes time to go to the recycling centre or charity shop, or to find a new home for unused toys.

An easy way to recycle old toys is to have a yard or garage sale.

By recycling more and throwing away less we can reduce the amount of waste being added to landfill sites like this one.

It's estimated that post-Christmas, each family throws away an extra five bags of rubbish. Much of this is packaging from presents and toys. A UK company called The Less Packaging Company is working with various toy producers to create better, more eco-friendly packaging.

Careful shopping

A lot of waste can be avoided by all of us being careful consumers. If we think about what we're buying and how it's packaged, we can make informed choices about our role in the waste mountain. Sometimes, choosing not to buy something because it's got too much wasteful packaging sends a strong message to the makers. If you do buy something with lots of packaging, make sure you recycle it carefully. Most recycling centres around the country now take polystyrene, hard plastics and cardboard. If you're not sure where your local recycling centre is, contact your local council offices.

SHOP TO CHANGE THE WORLD

The labels on the box will tell you where a product is made. It will also give you information about who made it and whether the product uses recycled materials or is eco-friendly. The best labels will also tell you how to safely dispose of or recycle the item once you've finished with it.

CHAPTER 4

HEALTHY WORK AND PLAY

The toy industry is growing all the time as more and more new ideas and products hit the shelves. It's a dynamic, fast-paced industry which campaigners say still has a lot to do to catch up in terms of worker health, environmental protection, waste management and, perhaps most importantly, safe toys. You'll learn that consumer concerns can change things and that people power can make a difference to the supply chain.

Dangerous toys?

A lot of research has been done into the effects on children of violent video games or even toy swords and guns. Some people think these kinds of toys should be banned or perhaps have age limits on them. What do you think? Do you think that children should be able to play with plastic guns? Is it just harmless fun or could there be more serious effects?

Should children be allowed to play with toy guns and weapons?.

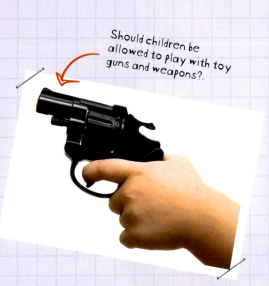

Many toy companies are responding to the growing parental fears about toy, weapons and violent video games. They now have child **psychologists** and child development experts working for them. This helps the companies to ensure that the toys they produce are not harmful to a child's developing sense of who they are.

Toy marketing

Each time you turn on the TV, you will see adverts for toys. In the adverts, the children are happy and excited and that might make you want the toy too. But are you being manipulated by the advert and the toy companies? Are you being presented with an artificial idea of how happy the toy will make you? What do you know about the company who made the toy? Will you still want it if it's made by child labour?

Some people think that playing with toy weapons may encourage children to think that violence is an acceptable way of solving problems, but others argue that it is a natural part of children's development.

SHOP TO CHANGE THE WORLD

Remember the power you have and that you can shop to change the world. It's easy to buy toys from companies who treat their workers well and pay a fair rate. It's also easy to avoid buying toys from companies that use child workers. Do an online search or check out one of the pressure groups listed on page 47.

Playing games with family and friends helps to develop children's imagination and key skills, such as counting.

37

MAKING CHANGES

Some of the biggest issues in the toy industry supply chain remain sweatshop labour and poor working conditions. In Far Eastern and Chinese toy factories, workers still report regular burns from **soldering irons** and electric shocks from old hair dryers used to set glue. They also still have to work with unmarked chemicals and suffer the consequences to their health. So what's being done to change this and improve each part of the toy industry supply chain?

International co-operation

Governments and international law-makers are trying to make a difference but, as we now know, everyone in the supply chain from the toy companies to consumers has a part to play in improving things.

The toy industry is regulated by the International Council of Toy Industries (ICTI) and then the government laws of each country apply to different stages of the supply chain. This means that if the toy is made in China, the factory conditions have to **comply with** Chinese law. If the toy is then sold in the UK, it has to follow the rules and regulations that the UK has for toy safety.

Soldering irons used in the toy industry can cause nasty burns if used incorrectly or without the correct safety equipment.

Industry campaign

The ICTI aims to improve working conditions and environmental protection, to promote ethical manufacturing of toys and ensure that people work in safe conditions. It has a **code of practice** which it promotes across the industry and all the way along the supply chain. Companies who sign this code agree to make sure that worker safety and the environment are their top priorities.

Part of the ICTI's demands is that all chemicals used in the toy supply chain are labelled. It also wants systems in place in each factory to protect workers who are working with **solvents**. Things are improving in the bigger factories but there are so many thousands of smaller factories, spread all over the world, that monitoring and change takes a very long time.

The ICTI campaigns for workers' safety in the toy industry.

Artisans Angkor was set up in Cambodia in 1999 to revive traditional craft skills in the country and help young people like these to find work in their home villages.

SHOP TO CHANGE THE WORLD

You can check which companies have signed up to the ICTI's CARE campaign which promotes ethical practices along the toy supply chain by going to www.icti-care.org and clicking on the retailer button. This will tell you which companies are committed to changing things for the better.

A CHILDHOOD FOR EVERYONE?

Imagine not being able to sit and play or just run around in the sunshine because you've got to go to work. It's a shocking idea, isn't it? In the UK, having a job might mean doing a paper round or doing extra jobs around the house for some pocket money. But as we've learned, for millions of children all over the world, childhood isn't a carefree time for play and fun; it's a daily grind to earn money.

Worldwide campaign

It's estimated that today, there are more than 200 million children trapped in child labour. Some of these are involved in the toy industry. In 1992, the International Programme on the Elimination of Child Labour (IPEC) was launched. Brazil, India, Indonesia, Kenya, Turkey and Thailand all signed the original agreement. IPEC focuses solely on child workers and today works in over 80 countries worldwide.

The use of child labour is still a big problem in countries such as India; but the IPEC is working to improve the lives of child workers around the world.

40

Some child workers have benefitted from projects that have been set up to help them, such as these classes at an education centre in Sialkot, Pakistan, which are funded by a company that manufactures footballs.

What can be done?

Campaigners say it will take governments, companies and consumers to all play their part to stop the use of child workers. In 1989, the United Nations created the Convention on the Rights of the Child. This powerful and very important document sets out what each child is entitled to. Each child has a right to be healthy, secure and safe, have an education and not be exploited. Governments where children work need to ensure that children's human rights are respected. Campaign groups point out that other governments can help by putting pressure on countries such as Uzbekistan that use child labour by not trading with them.

A moving problem?

Whilst child labour may be going down in some countries such as China, the figures suggest that the issue is moving to a new region. An international campaign in the 1990s helped to lower the number of children in the football-making industry, but these children then moved, in some cases, to other industries such as the brick kilns. Four in ten African children now work. Is this a new country to target?

SHOP TO CHANGE THE WORLD

Every year, June 12th is the United Nations World Day Against Child Labour. On this day, governments and youth organisations from around the world gather together to discuss and agree what to do to **eliminate** child labour. Find out what events are happening near you at www.ilo.org.

FAIR PLAY AND BIG BUSINESS

With consumers starting to demand more information about the supply chain of the toys they buy, big businesses are starting to take notice. Small independent toy companies are leading the way with changes throughout, from design to manufacturing and working conditions to packaging. Knowing that the toy was made in a safe and responsible way is becoming more important to consumers today, and the big companies are slowly starting to catch up.

Shops may offer a bewildering choice of toys to customers, but knowing more about how a toy is produced can help you decide how to spend your money.

For children, not by children

Babipur is just one of a number of small, ethical and responsible toy companies that value workers and ensure that each link in the supply chain is as ethical as possible. All the toys it sells for babies and children are made from **organic** materials and don't have any chemicals in them. The company only works with factories who look after their workers and don't work with any producer who uses child labour. Visit the website at www.babipur.co.uk.

Getting informed

It's easy to source healthy, natural toys which are sweatshop-free and eco-friendly. Consumer websites such as www.ethicalconsumer.org offer a wealth of ideas and information so you can be an ethical and responsible, consumer. Other websites where you can buy toys that don't cost the earth in terms of resources or waste include www.ilovetoys.co.uk. On this site, you can buy amazing toys that are eco-friendly, ethical, fair trade and local. This means the company isn't creating extra pollution by sending the toys halfway around the planet.

Electronic toys are a big success with today's children. If you do a little research before you buy these toys, you can be a responsible and ethical shopper.

SHOP TO CHANGE THE WORLD

As a toy consumer, you can play your part in the purchasing chain and help to make a real difference to the toy industry. People are looking for companies that are good to their employees and to the environment. You can try to avoid companies with poor records of child labour or poor environmental care. High quality eco-friendly and sustainable products exist already and with your help in being a responsible consumer, there will be more and more.

43

SHOP TO CHANGE THE WORLD

It takes lots of resources, people and energy to make a single toy and the supply chain that starts with design and ends with purchase is very complicated indeed. The issues of working conditions, child labour, environmental protection and toy safety are the key challenges facing this massive global industry and ourselves as consumers. The good news is there are companies and people out there helping to make a difference and working to shut down sweatshops. Do you want to be part of that change?

Power to the people!

People power, whether it's led by consumers or the workers themselves, really can make a difference. Remember the Firestone rubber plantation in Liberia on page 29? Well, that union joined a larger one called the Agricultural Workers Union of Liberia and now the workers have powerful people speaking up for them. The union leaders voice the workers' concerns and stand up for them against poor working conditions and unrealistic targets.

In 2012, thousands of workers in Indonesia went on a protest march to demand better wages.

In developing countries, many parents work long hours to send their children to school.

Changing from the top?

If the problems in the toy industry supply chain are really going to be solved, it will take the will of big businesses and governments. You can do your bit by only buying fair trade, sweat-free, eco-friendly toys and saying no to toy companies that do not pay a fair wage to their workers. Toy companies may want to make as much money as possible and encourage customers to buy by keeping toy prices low. But at some point, people pay and, as we've learned, that usually means children working for nothing and adults working in terrible conditions. If you're fed up with the lack of fair play, then make your voice heard and shop to change the world.

We're all responsible if things stay as they are and we can all play our part in changing them for the better. Who wants to start playing fair?

SHOP TO CHANGE THE WORLD

You could join a campaign group that works to change conditions for children and sweatshop workers. There are many online campaigns and lots of information out there. See page 47 for more details.

GLOSSARY

chemicals   a substance created by a chemical process

code of practice   guidelines that workers and managers agree to follow

comply with   follow or meet a standard

confinement   kept locked away, enclosed

consumer   a person who buys products, such as toys, for personal use

eco-friendly   environmentally friendly, products that are not harmful to the environment

economy   the business of a country

eliminate   to get rid of

ethical consumer   shopper who buys fair trade goods and who thinks of the morals behind a purchase

ethical practices   business chains with good morals and high standards

exploited   abused

exporters   companies who sell products abroad

fair trade   fairly sharing profits along the supply chain

human trafficking   when people are transported and forced to work for others, often for little (or no) money

organic   natural, chemical-free

petitions   official letters requesting actions

profit   the money a business earns after expenses have been subtracted

psychologists   experts in how people think

raw materials   materials or substances used in the primary production or manufacturing of a product

respiratory   relating to the process of breathing

retailer   a shop or business that usually sells goods made elsewhere

soldering iron   a tool for joining metals together

solvents   substances, usually liquids, capable of dissolving other substances

suicide   the act of taking one's own life intentionally

supply chain   the route products take from the source to the consumer

sustainable   possible to continue, without long-term side effects

sweatshop   factories with poor working conditions and low pay

toxic   poisonous; harmful to health

trade union   an organisation that protects the interests of workers

ventilation   circulation of fresh air

FOR MORE INFORMATION

Books

Fiction
Boys without Names, Kashmira Sheth, HarperCollins, 2011.

Gopal's family live in a tiny Indian village; poverty forces them to travel to Mumbai to seek work. In this moving book, Kashmira Sheth takes the reader into the world of child labour and exposes the horrors suffered by millions of children around the world.

Non-fiction
Real Life Stories: Child Worker, Catherine Chambers, ticktock Media Ltd., 2005

Just the facts: Child Labour, Kaye Stearman, Heinemann Library, 2004

Websites

If you're interested in joining a pressure group or finding out more about being a super consumer, check out the following websites:

www.dosomething.org
This is a great website for teenagers to get involved in issues you care about.

www.sweatfree.org/shopping
Explore this website and see what this charity is doing to assist sweatshop workers around the world.

www.betterworldshopper.org
This website rates companies on their social and environmental responsibility.

www.greenpeace.org
Check out this website and find out about environmental issues and what you can do to make a difference.

www.kidsforsavingearth.org
This website is all about how you can help to protect our planet.

INDEX